# Uprooted Orchid

Sarah Joy Thompson

## Dedication

This poetry collection is an acknowledgement of grief and a celebration of joy. Herein the messages become documentary, witnesses of personal experience, and love. I dedicate this book to the many individuals who have touched my life. In memory of Lewis Reynolds Goff.

# Contents

# Prologue

## Perceptions of Despair

When we are young the dark
can be frightening for things
inconceivable are surely
lurking there. We make believe
we are mommies and daddies
bouncing dolls in our arms,
bringing life into the world,
doctors, vets, and nurses
bandaging our teddies' limbs,
caring for helpless creatures.

On a car ride home we look
at the low hanging
moon on the horizon,
turn over questions
in our innocent minds,
"What are we going to do
if the moon runs out
of floating power?"
We are so small
and need hands to hold
us, to hold syllables
we clap into the night.

We cannot even fathom
illnesses of the lungs,
damaged cells, genetic
cards dealt on the table,
the loss of a parent.
We cannot feign
capability to navigate
the unknown space
with the lights turned off.

With age we learn
to kneel in the fields,
reposition the stars
and their cosmic patterns,
because without the dark
we would not notice
the merciful light,
the found poems.

# Let the smallness, the nothingness find me

Waiting out the pandemic, I want to shapeshift into a bumblebee
Collect nectar in the Mexican petunia outside an artist's front door
Inspire her watercolor sketches, purple petals taking form
Black and yellow abdomen, lacey wings on mixed media paper

Or I could be a poet's potted orchid, magenta blooms, sangria lips
I'd hold up my flowers for her during winter's coldest months
Shed in March, when signs of life appear on branches in the open air
Enough green pushing through, not so fragile, hope for her again
She could trim my stems down, press my flowers
Between pages, holding on to life coming in cycles

When tragedies in the news infect my bloodstream
Increased harassment targeted at Asians during Covid-19 outbreaks
A call to stop the hate pumps like fire through my veins
Oh, I'd rather be an infant, innocent, in my Filipina mother's arms
She could grasp me tight in the fragile moments of human nature
Before ink and memories fade from paper

Or I could be as lonely as a drifting grain of silt, disconnected
From the noise of the media, pulled swiftly to the shoreline
Where it all started, life developing at the cusp of water and sand
I'd join a mass of frothy ocean spume, pulsing with the heartbeat
Of the sea, a ritual of the memorable breaths
Returning home to the earth's womb

# A Night in March

This is the only way
To work in small patches
Mopping up muddied surfaces
After footprints from toddler shoes
And doggy paws have designed
A pirate map with landmarks leading
From back door to stairway

The dishwasher is filled and turned on
Worn clothes placed into the washer
Set to a heavy cycle, *swoosh, swoosh*
Clean clothes removed from dryer
Folded into an empty basket
Art materials packed up, shoved
Into any closet with space
The little boy fed, bathed
Kissed, tucked into bed

Around here household duties
Are hummed into quiet meditations
The inner self holding conversations
My positive thoughts are dialed in
And to keep my sanity, I progress
From low hums to full-fledged songs
*Click, clang, thump* looking for serenity

## Lipstick and Pajamas

when pandemic fatigue sinks in, there is nowhere lower
to stoop, the magic fades into remote work, suburban life
depression becomes unbearable, there is no one
around to notice I'm trying to hold it together

go ahead, I whisper to myself in the mirror
and take the precautions to boost my mental health
do yoga in my bedroom, walk laps around the yard
move my body, attempt to eat healthy food
go ahead, I give myself permission, pin up my hair, put bright
violet lipstick on, change out of my flannel PJs
wear some jewelry, don an ironed dress, floral chiffon
move some more, dance around the living room

by choice I am more than a cold silhouette in despair
I am a woman capable of fighting back, gaining desire
for life back, and I embrace the art of bowing to a belief
or cause larger than myself, I take my awkward body
lean into the dance of contribution
until things start easing into a new normal

I squeeze my toddler tight, tell my husband 100 times a day

how much I love him, reach out to kindred souls

who detest the hopelessness, the news outlets

imagine they've lost loved ones and their heroes too

imagine that humanity is not altogether torn

there is merely a collective emptiness that needs filling

## Innocent Then

Part of my childhood was a long white dining table
over a dozen seats, dustpans, dish basins, Baguio brooms
I wore my sisters' hand-me-down clothes, slept in homemade
bunkbeds in shared rooms, shared belongings, shared chores

For a time, we had a big house, yellow roof, in Suello Village
with an island table in the kitchen, mother taught us how
to light the gas oven, bake, fend for ourselves, the *Joy of Cooking*
and *Mrs. Fields Cookie Book* stained with pastry crust, batter, dough

I would sneak out to the brick chimney on the side of the house
climb each dainty rebar rung, peer out at the rolling fog, pine trees
I felt the wind as a young girl feels, innocently, perched on the high
crown I'd wait for shivers, goose bumps, a sense of excitement

The big house was nice, but it had a wraparound fence
that separated us missionary children from the outside world
our homeschooling was a bore, we played childish pranks
like Harry Houdini, tied one brother up, pinned him down

He lost a tooth, biting knotted fabric, trying to free himself

those moments, wild and rambunctious occasionally

rise at holiday get-togethers when it's late and some

have had too much to drink, some fight and leave

Others stay, seek forgiveness, "I'm sorry for being so mean

to you when we were kids, wish I would have loved you better"

## Little did we know

I receive news on the phone dad is at his worst, lungs failing
I put my toddler in the playroom, hold my knees to chest
Murmur a litany of moody dispositions into a pillow

Just yesterday I had on little white and pink sneakers
Trying to keep up with dad's big strides as he carried
Bible, magazines, and umbrella door to door
He was teaching us, "Do unto others as you would have them
Do unto you" and "Always say your bedtime prayers"
Full of preaching, a heart fated to serve like Francis
The Philippines his Assisi, offering Bible studies to inmates
Bringing relief goods to typhoon victims, praying
For the ill in hospice care, hosting parties for those
With nowhere to go for Noche Buena

Just yesterday I imagined his heart larger than his fists
Measureless, and in my first memory of him he is tall
So tall he blocks the whole doorway of a room and ducks
His head down to get through the door, then in illness
He changes from being a giant to being someone so frail
Propped up on pillows, I can almost carry him in my arms

Just yesterday my older siblings and I were whispering

"How much longer do you think dad has left to live?"

And we proceeded to buy tickets home for his 70th birthday

We were startled when he walked with us on the beach

His 6' 3" frame hunched down, weighing under 120 pounds

Skin clinging around lanky bones, frailer than ever


Just yesterday he admitted he missed mornings

When we could share a cup of coffee and a slice

Of mom's homemade bread around the kitchen table

Cracking jokes with his kids, making fun of each

Other like no one was watching, he signed up

For Facebook at the start of the Covid-19 lockdowns

Wanting access to our lives, more ways to be in touch


I begin touch typing in low light to process what's next

Ask my siblings how we will uncover enough resilience

To handle the decline of this man who is such

A seasoned practitioner of hiding his pain


On my last phone calls with dad, I listen to him wheeze

Midsentence, then painfully inhale between words

Oxygen tank at his bedside, he should be resting

But he prays for my day, sends me off with a blessing

## Goodbyes on video calls

I.

After a hospital visit induced by an intense flare up –
Backlash from COPD, irreversible damage to the lungs
Dad goes home, goes to sleep, he does not wake up

We turn to cellphone video calls, through screens
Our mother's eyes are frantic, our youngest brothers
Are powerless in Baguio's foggy grasp, ever so alone
They trudge through this nightmare's haze

Lockdown in Baguio, Philippines
International flights banned
I stay awake with my siblings
Another night and another

The group call drops
A visiting nurse helps mom
With his diaper

Worried about oral bacteria
Nurse gets a cup of mouthwash
Dips a strip of gauze
Cleanses dad's mouth
She removes a dental bridge
From his bottom molars

His deep unconscious state
Does not change


II.
We barely breathe through painful
Video chat vigils on Zoom
Or Facebook Messenger
Calling is the closest thing
To holding each other


From the Philippines
To Australia and America
Our tear ducts and faces
Swell, "Can't sleep," I say
"Can't sleep either," they echo


III.
On the fourth day of his deep sleep
A nurse tells us to watch for signs
Of terminal restlessness
A twitch could be a decrease in oxygen
Panting, shallow breaths, periods
Of no breathing for a minute or so
Could be alerting end-of-life

"Can't watch you like this
Anymore," mom says to him
"Can't watch either," we echo

Matthew, age 12, throws himself
Against concrete walls, hands in fists
Flailing and pounding overhead
Kieran, 16, holds it together
Brings phone closer to dad's face, and we
Muster up courage, say what we need to say

## What Remains

Wake up, you've been sleeping
Too much in a routine
Not loving, not experiencing

Our father taught us that
When a pain so grave
Aches in our rib cages

How could we not have loved
Have experienced
To this man, our first love

Everything was in walking distance
And now he will walk, walk, walk
Sweet restless somnambulist

He has gone now
On his biggest adventure

## Reclaiming the Narrative

"sadness is just as beautiful as love, it is proof that love existed and
nothing to be ashamed of"

– artist and sister, Stephanie C. L. Goff

Part 1.

Before I approach a masked woman

I wonder if she also keeps one –

a list that reveals her private imperfections


I've got spider veins on my thighs

coarse hair frequently prone to frizzing

unpredictable eruptions of the pain held within


I lost my father to chronic obstructive pulmonary disease

when I was 28, thinking he'd stay around longer

to nourish relationships with his kids, grandkids


I wept for days in front of my 2-year-old

battled to get out of bed and eat, stopped tidying

up the house, walked and drove directionless


What is the role for having a body

to scrutinize in the dark

disorderly, disruptive… if we learn nothing

Masked woman, let us air our lists

so they lose their power, learn to love

a part of the self we could not reach before


Let us unravel and undo the strings to unearth

the original shards of our distinctiveness, until the being

is morphed, and our remnants are poetry


Part 2.

It comes from a painful place

finding grace, in the dark aftermath

to say, I forgive you for leaving me too early


A broken spirit incased in a fragile frame

an uprooted orchid

with no anchor to a tree or shrub


Mourning your death encompassed

all my lifetime's worth of emptiness

as I watched the stronghold


Of my childhood dreams

and an ill man I love

burn to the ground

Now that so much of my being
has been destroyed, what should I do
with these charred memories

Sweep through the ashes with faint hands
find any piece of salvageable charcoal
to hold between my fingertips

Press it against the page of a sketchbook
tap, tap, tap, tap, tap…
attempt to draw a new world

## Midnight Folk Hits

At birth I had no religion
just a folk song tucked
neatly in my vocal cords

Tossing my body
in the wrong direction
at night, a discomfort
makes sleep difficult

Often, this impetus
to form melancholy lyrics
comes at odd hours
when our condo neighbors
are asleep or in quietude

The songs want to move in me
want to travel from artery
to muted guitar strings
like possibilities born into a vast
story, waiting to exist
as if they could say to me
start somewhere close to home

and never for a moment forget
how your ancestors transcribed you
gifting sentient music to
your deep-rooted soul

Crying sometimes accompanies
these songs, memories
of loving a deceased man
how he left after ignored warnings
with just a handful of what
he sang, yet no chords

With obnoxious alto voice
untrained and pitchy
I scribble out fragments
what I remember
of his songs, branches
from which I fell

## Forests Born Under Sky Dreams

When the early whispers of autumn
Fly gaily through our home
On the wind's strings
In small, delicate symphonies
We spill our bodies on the bed
Crawl between freshly washed cotton sheets
And twist our limbs into unorganized knots
We nibble on the last of our summer frenzies
Memories of berry picking
In warm July and August
Trying to taste the garden-fresh
Sweet juices of the raspberries
Blueberries, blackberries
That burst on our tongues
Between teeth and roused taste buds

But before we swallow autumn's bounty
Hot spiced ciders, baked goods with cloves
Cinnamon, nutmeg, allspice
Before the fall gifts her delicate presents
Floods of cinnabar, fire opal, honey topaz
To the rolling forests along Skyline Drive
Backbone of Shenandoah National Park
Let us kiss with our words in bed, until
Our tongues are tickled and pulsing

Let the moans escape from our lungs

Vibrating into the shadows

Of the year's last summer nights

## True Like Time

There was a bit of calm before the traffic
But the evening rush hour mirrored us
Frantic, drunk, lusting
For high seas in the summer
Wanting to be enormously wild
Like innocent children clutching
The language of untainted joy
In our mouths, on our tiny tongues
Small hands holding salt water
Shimmering specks of light
When we could inhale, exhale
Time... and youth was a typo
Repeated too frequently
Omitted too easily

Youth became a fragment
Elusive like words we forgot to say
Or didn't repeat often enough
I love you I love you I love you
A run-on sentence
Then a full stop
Time... all lives so fragile

Building my first ofrenda

For Dia de los Muertos in 2020

To place my father's picture upon

Put things into perspective

No matter how we try to suppress

The notion of getting older, duller

Moments pour out of our eyeballs

With a few drinks

At family gatherings


And we feel tricked by the minutes

And we cannot stop time

## Waiting for Winter

Sliding door ajar

listening to December winds

pick up speed as the last yellowed leaves

outside our window lose their grip

and scantily clad branches

form proscenium arches

botanical theatres

framing this gray show

beyond the glass


As I step outside

the approaching season

comes with icy breath

touching the neck

biting extremities, my fingers go numb

alternating between one hand

in the pocket of my parka

one hand around the dog leash


My body halted

by the unpredictable cold

I feel so much like an old tree

which has been through landslides

the soil shaken at my roots

almost toppled over

my bark deliberately invaded

by lichen and moss


But still I choose to grow upright

splash grounding water on my face

something rose-scented with murumuru

to remind me of my siblings in California

resting a hand against

a younger sister's cheek

to produce perfect liquid lines

of eyeliner on soft eyelids

or a troop of us frolicking

through trails that lead

to Redwood fairy rings

or the hollows of giant trees

staying up late in the kitchen

to talk things over

to talk over each other

to laugh, be heard, be seen

At least there is reminiscing

to make our winter

not so cold after all

## Each Evident Season

*"Everything repeats. The seasons, the patterns of day and night, babies being born and parents dying, two people discovering each other's bodies: everything, large and small, has happened before — or almost."*

*— The Poet's Companion*

Your waterproof winter boots

Meet puddles and soggy leaves

Bounding along the trailways

As your wide eyes seem

To check mine constantly

I find it funny how the earth

Is mine to see anew each day

Through your gaze, brave one


There you are testing

Your knees and stomach

Against the ground

When you fall and wail

Then pull yourself together

Toting nature treasures along

Fallen leaves in every phase

Handfuls of acorns, pinecones

A crooked walking stick

Sedimentary rocks

I once was like you, and here
Is the circle game I discover
Myself in now, wherein
You put all your trust in me
Asking me to hold your
Noteworthy possessions
And want them all
Accept them all, love them all

If my eyes were lenses
They would photograph
The bold new outlook
In your steel blue eyes
Speckled with mystery, light
So we can attempt to
Fathom, together
This great chain of love
That makes the seasons
Follow each other
And the world go round

# Lupinus Havardii, Big Bend Bluebonnet Dreams

In isolation, thoughts desire a breakaway
appear like a pile of poetry magnets
in a metal tray, waiting, wanting to make
sense of being stuck at home, ending the year
with a to-do list that comes with its own anxiety
first let us do the laundry, wash bathroom rugs
scrub the tubs, toilets, and sinks
take out trash bags, cleanse, cleanse

While I'm trying to decipher the year's sum
of congested emotions, caught at the intersection
of mind, pure human emotion, and the rush
all I ask is that you pinch me in the morning
if we are still held to our bed by gravity
craving the sleep our worn bodies need
for the push of day, the breakthroughs
to take place at the threshold of a new year

Remind me in the fashion of planning a road trip
that most of my favorite days begin
with rumors of Chisos Basin wildflowers
driving away from city and nest
flying my heart out the window – a busy kite
scintillating in southwest Texas breeze

# A Tent Pitched Near the Guadalupe River

No doubt the sound of moving water
carries well along limestone bluffs
as clouds pour into the river
and soil just rained upon
becomes the earth's perfume.

It's trifling to hold still in a tent
when my day's mission is to go
outdoors to answer bird calls
twirling here and there with binoculars
catching glimpses of the canyon wren
turkey vulture, common raven
black-crested titmouse, carolina chickadee
northern cardinal, white-winged dove.

I try my best, wait impatiently with journal
for clear skies to travel my way, think of resting
like languid prairie verbena or golden-eye phlox
roots fixed, petals and leaves dressed in droplets
make believe no plans were interrupted.

Even wildflowers have undefined stories.

## Visiting My Ilongga Mother

Ginger, garlic, and onion residue linger
Under my fingernails after
Grated and minced ingredients
Are thrown into the pot

Monggo soup simmers with coconut milk
Smells that remind me of mother's cooking
Or how she enfolded us with life lessons
In a nurturing kitchen environment

This is the loveliness of cooking
Being able to traverse space and time
While preparing a simple meal
A cultural hand-me-down

And always sitting back with anticipation
Trying and experimenting, perfecting the recipe
With a teaspoon of turmeric or curry powder
To appeal to my acquired tastes of aging

Mother's recipes still live in my mind, in my kitchen
As I revisit the bridge that joins me to her bones

## Mother's Day, 2021

She'll talk about her kids, grandkids
to keep her mind off dad's passing
gray hair pulled back into a ponytail
flyaway strands frame her face

She looks tired, she's let herself go
"I'm in limbo" she'll confide

My stubborn mother, who never complained
about baby blues or post-partum depression
after having twelve children
accepting her stepchildren
still says "You children are my life"
never "I gave up my life for you"

She poured out her soul onto each of us
like drops of water into potting soil
nurturing the seeds, the buds, the flowers
of an immaculate garden

Now, I wish I could put my arms
around her worn, slouched body
wish I could bring her flowers

when she feels so alone

say "Don't worry about dad,

he's probably having a fresh cup of coffee

where good men go in the afterlife"

## I'll send small presents and a poem on August 5th

Dear mom, I know you're sentimental this time of year
another lonesome birthday without dad to sit beside you
mom, you should take care of yourself, I advise
although there is no magic word that can slip
from my lips to make you less lonely falling asleep

What is it like loving a ghost when you haven't
heard from him in a long time, do you wait on
your side of the bed, leave him space
if he should sneak into the house, does a ghost
turn all the lights out, take off his shoes
get under the covers gently, breathe next to you
does a ghost make you warm until morning

I'd like to fly just to see you, keep you company
watch cheesy romantic movies, eat Filipino food
pamper you, buy a nice present, sing Happy Birthday
distract you from wishing you could bring
the dead home, distract you from losing sleep
again and again, with arms empty again

Since I can't be there, I offer some small gifts
for your special day, but before you receive them

first, fold into a child's pose, press forehead

against the earth, start new cycles, it's time

for new desires and pursuits to push through


Let the late sun linger on your fingertips

acknowledge the one you miss most

thank him for the memories, warmth

think of the children you and he made

together, and the grandchildren you have now

each unique individual a testimony of love

## Tantrums

So here is the other side of the coin
another facet of motherhood, the tumultuous
fury in a toddler's screams, still learning
that his actions affect others. Where are the
books, documentaries, podcasts about dealing
with onslaughts of emotional stress?

How uproarious, how many, how long the outbursts?
Crying on the floor of a store because I said no
to eye-catching plastic toys or candy pumped
with artificial colors and high fructose corn syrup.
Mood interrupted because someone else pressed
the button on the elevator door first. At what age
the compassion, the character, the reasoning?

Call it early childhood development or a burden
in my hands, as I try to carry and nurture this boy. Oh
the blood pumping headaches, red eyes, anxiety. Yet
the real battle is in resisting my urge to raise my voice,
not stooping to his level. This child is making sure
I learn more than my share of controlling my anger.
Regulating my emotions, no need for my own quickened
heart rate, hey, I'm getting to know myself.

How heavenly this, finding a little voice offering

the merited tenderness needed to calm the child

in both of us. Perhaps this introspection has saved

mothers the world over, pausing to ask the soul

what to gift her. Here she tells me not to force my motions,

lift limbs against gravity, fight the unreasonable fight,

yell as a last resort. But act with patience, slow down,

ground my feet to the earth. Take deep, restoring breaths

until I am filled with enough forgiveness, willing

to hug a troublemaker, press his ear to my heart,

wave a temper tantrum peace flag. Truce.

## Containers

Rectangle container made of plastic

on my table, the apple and orange slices

devoured now, bottom showing white stains

signs of wear and tear from our dishwasher

rectangle container has no heirloom status

an old housewarming gift, overused


I strive every day for my life

to mean more than this container's

to love something larger than myself

I wish for the stories I contain

to be upcycled for other journeys

to be passed down to my children


I imagine the narrative shapes in me

how I'm often drawn to the triangles

the most structurally stable shape

pyramids endured through the years

ancient civilizations erected these

temples by stacking stone upon stone

the Pyramid of the Sun in Mexico

the Great Pyramid of Giza in Egypt

There is the triangle of my family
my husband, our son, me, we put our minds
together to raise a boisterous modern boy
lift him up for shoulder rides, purposely let leaves
tickle his head when we walk under bushy branches
he invents new purposes for objects, hot water bottles
in winter are warm hugs, we squeeze him to our hearts

Then another persistent triangle which stems
from my lineage, dad, mom, me, an ancestry
intertwined with Filipina, Scottish, English roots
I place my parents on a pedestal, no matter how
far they are always with me, mine to keep
through the years, architectural wonders

Also, there is my spiritual longing
raised in a Christian household while
drawn to pre-colonial medicines, beliefs
animism in the Cordillera Region of the Philippines
the earth goddess Pachamama in the Andes
Mexico's manifestations of nature, cosmology
but I have no name for the shape of this longing

## On Vincent Cooper's "Zarzamora"

When I picked it up the book was so easy to lift

It wouldn't even register on my digital bathroom scale


After reading the poem

"Some Other Time Then", pages 52-55

I placed *Zarzamora* under my pillow

My hands and lungs weighted down

By different versions of a

      "Syrian boy washed ashore. Dead"


My own inner sorrows still gasping

While I felt a punch in the gut, called out

One of the people scrolling

      "quickly through their cellphone

      social media timelines,

      so their meals or mood wouldn't be ruined"


Are my ambitions upon re-entering the world

After life in quarantine so pathetic

That I make excuses and ignore the tragedies around me

Become distracted by planning weekend activities

Or get lost in a void of working and buying all the arbitrary

Material possessions I want delivered to my doorstep?

Really, why do we waste away here
If we're not learning how much we can
Love, do, be better
In all the sleepless nights I counted
From reading this book
I felt a suppression that could not be replicated
A desperate prayer for redemption

If Vincent's inner captive
Could smile within those dark walls
It is all the proof I need
The art that eats you
Can also heal you
A glimmer of promise
A letting go of inhibition

And that is why I sing
Because of the tender hopes for this world
Echoed in another poet's past darkness
A reflection of myself

## And Often I Wish to Return

If I were a chord today, then a C major
singing Cielito Lindo to the streets
of Oaxaca's Zócalo on my last night
before departure, taking in the couples salsa dancing
swaying, each scene a kiss under a lamp light, a poem
that writes itself

The chord sometimes speaks with the voice
of a seasoned southern Mexican tour guide
showing off her cultura y folklorico
weaving in and out of stories told in
Zapotec, Mixtec, Mazatec
her third eye understanding

I'd like to sit in conversation a little longer
as she asks in some other tongue, where
do you want to go next?

Oaxaca, Oaxaca, no let me say it again
Huaxyacac, Huaxyacac, she seems so dreamy
to me still, the water of Hierve el Agua lingers
on my palms, and the soil too of Monte Albán
and the Pueblos Mancomunados

I can't wait to revisit her ever immaculate

landscapes, her best foot forward, her dances

her smiles, Huaxyacac, Huaxyacac

missing her calms the summer nights

## Paint Postulations, "Vendedora de Alcatraces"

I am inspiration sipped, swirled in glass, sweet, smoky
making paint water murky, saying what comes to mind
mostly silly sentiments and prose, until a line sticks out
and there is something for the artist to build on

He searches, reaches for paintbrush, dabs
bristles in pigments, strokes the outlines of
a maiden with almond oil skin, braids to her navel
carrying her basket full of calla lilies

She walks through the plaza, mind heavy
thoughts weighted down by nimbus clouds
praying under breath for rain, thunder showers
before noon in the delirious heat of summer

On the corners of her mouth a hunger
where visions of her kitchen at lunch hour
make her crave corn tortillas fresh from
the comal, dipped in secret salsa recipes

On her brow the determination to sell flowers

so she can go home to a strong man's brown hands

that will lift her blouse, uncover moist skin

beg her to stay for a steamy siesta de la tarde

# Frown Lines, A Portrait of Myself at 29

For my editor's photo I pose in our small living room
Arms folded as if to keep a lid on my excitement
Favorite black, V-neck dress with short sleeves
Dangling pear-shaped earrings, matching necklace
Hair down in natural waves, catching window light
Zoom in to my long oval face, wide offset smile
Brown almond eyes, framed by medium lashes
Nose slightly upturned at the tip, zoom even closer

Despite ceremoniously dabbing hydrating serum
Around my procerus region, that line by my left brow
Persists as a sign of focused, voracious reading
Face constantly in a book as a girl, as a woman
Falling asleep with books stacked by my pillow

Mary Pope Osborne's *Magic Tree House* series
Enhanced an early wanderlust in 8-year-old Sarah Joy
And by the time I reached my 20s I fully enjoyed
Discovering whimsical pueblos tucked in mountain chains
Different terrains under bare feet, fallen pine needles
Dressed in morning dew or basil branches
In a sweltering temazcal healing session

Then I found poets, who touched my pilgrim soul

Mary Oliver, Naomi Shihab Nye, Joy Harjo

I sat in foreign gardens and coffee shops, absorbing

So much of this beautiful planet in words and in person

The crease in my brow persisting, immersed in stories

## Voluminous Hair

A spirit that lives in my hair
pushes out regular old bobby pins
so I get fancy barrettes with tension bars
to hold fussy strands in place, I fatigue my triceps
as I fight to neatly section and pin it all up

She's a colicky baby at times, frizzing out
here, there, sensitive to cotton or polyester
which make her strands coarse and livid
during sleep, I try to restrict how I turn
only use a silk pillowcase at night

For the past year I've been improving
my hair routine, avoiding hot tools
experimenting with twists and braids
using all-natural shampoo, conditioner
no sulfates, parabens, or propylene glycol

I let the waves grow past collar bones
to the bottom of my breasts, dreaming
of lengths down to my belly button, but
I can't control my hair's intensity, it's me
against a spirited ego, mind of her own

## Conspicuous Table

We had some hiccups in that small San Antonio apartment
first place to ourselves, first serious relationship
I studied at the table cluttered with textbooks
dirty dishes, bowls of rice, soy sauce, sriracha shrine
hand towels and surface spray to clean up messes

Your love was distracted, felt digital even
no hands all over me like I craved, lusted for
when we stopped communicating, I would close
my eyes for minutes that turned into hours
revolving around breaths and mantras
sitting cross-legged, mind Lotus meditations

I was trying to think my way out
go back to the mountains, did someone say
mountains? you asked, but didn't plan
I saw you would continue to misunderstand me
if I stayed, freedom traded for a bone, a kennel
losing wild instincts, inhibited from screaming
excitedly at the night, walking with head down
heart limp, howls incapable of escaping

How long did you stare at the space where I

had left my mess, remnants of a naked woman

feral face covered in earth pigment, holding in

my art, a paper piñata, before you came after me?

# Faint traces

the muscle operator of my hands is a neat freak

can't stand to sit still or write when

toddler toys are strewn around creative spaces


when dog hair is visible under furniture

and vacuum is in reach, she cleans

to purify the energy in the room


I try to find a natural light source to write

but then the muscle operator sees

snake plants and orchids need watering


the dishwasher calls to be emptied

laundry in the dryer craves folding

more toys here, more there, and dog hair


it's as if the muscle operator wants

to stage a room in a way that allows

space for new growth, transfiguration


when the scene is set, she remembers

what it's like to find parts of the self

misplaced under mundane household things

the love songs pulled from a guitar

unearthed hours of talking and listening

warm bodies making biological discoveries

# Thoughts on Leaving

A little ache a type of homesickness
a longing I don't want to talk about
the stress and obsession of our move
as it all too soon approaches

The first time I packed my life into
a suitcase I was 19 years old
heading off for college, flying
from Cebu to Texas

Now I downsize again to move
to Ireland with my husband
a 3-year-old son, a baby in my belly
five suitcases amongst us

If emotion is something, its many
forms grow in gray fog around me
as we slowly chew our last meals
take-out food on a bare wooden floor
backs propped against the wall

Our condo stands here empty
soon without a family like ours

no toddler to jump on the backs

of sofas and run into rooms

before baths and bedtime stories

no dog to curl up at the feet

of tired parents once blankets

have been pulled over shoulders


What I've come to understand about

moving across towns, countries, oceans

is that it doesn't feel easy at the onset

for the heart or the body, so much

is left unsaid in that kind of letting go

## Nature Offerings

When pandemic precautions were easing up a little
I would put on my most comfortable maternity clothes
Take my toddler out to the countryside, where we'd gaze
At red and green tractors slowly going
Up the hills and stalling traffic, their muddy
Wheels spinning in hypnotic rotations
Sometimes plump new lambs would peek
Through hedges and shrubby gorse clusters

We found solace in visiting gardens
Looking for seeds that grounded themselves
Micro leaves that pushed toward sunlight
Answering the therapeutic call to step outside
Observe beauty abounding in plant shapes, shadows
Or smell clippings of pine and sprigs of clover

A small naturalist following in my footsteps
Same nature awe as me, my toddler would squat
Look more closely at things on the ground
Exclaim in proclamations of childish wonder
"Look, mommy, a mushroom,
Let's sit here and watch it grow"

I felt a world of support while walking into woods

Chasing waterfalls with my caring boy

Sensing that his love for nature and nurture

Would gently nudge him into the role of big brother

To baby number two growing in my womb


Forest bathing became our way of hope

Quiet meditations, the possibility of simply

Being, without definition or goal

## Anatomy of a Dress

My belly is outgrowing my regular clothes
and as my breasts grow too, I feel a tumor
above my left nipple. At this rate, I may not
be able to nurse my second son. Once a body

capable of sustenance, my body is now a source of fear.
I put on an old, favorite dress. It's not a maternity dress
but I want to keep wearing it, or try until the side seams
hugging my belly give out and the fibers

struggle to retain their form. First a centimeter,
then an inch of raw fabric edges will expose
bare skin and it won't be so neat when I haven't got
any needles or thread to patch up the blend

of cotton, modal, spandex. No way to prevent
my skin from spilling through.

Ta Da! says flesh – baby belly galore.

## Diagnosis

I was 38 weeks pregnant, arms trembling around my belly

As if I could protect my unborn son from this news

His age would almost mark the duration of treatments

September baby, it felt like the movies

Fighting not to breakdown emotionally

Nodding my head numbly, while

The breast care specialist revealed

Results of the biopsy and breast imaging


He spoke unfamiliar terms that flew over my head

I looked up at the ceiling trying to catch the words

Carcinoma, triple negative breast cancer

He mapped out my tumor, tapped pen on paper

At the options, more words, chemotherapy, surgery

Radiation therapy, follow up treatments


Then it was my turn to ask questions

"What will happen to my baby?" I choked

The confused mother in me crawled through

Warm tears came, they just rolled

Down my face into my mask

In the waiting room, calling cards, a pink booklet

On my lap *Understanding Breast Cancer*

Soon there were phone calls

## On Breath and Birth

Sa.  I look down at the boy wrapped snug against my chest

And say to him

Don't let me go alone

To and from the place that we know

To the place where we are waiting

Ta.  There is a bright light overhead

My eyes are shut, dry from empty tear ducts

I am giving up, tired and exhausted

Everyone is yelling "He's almost here, he's almost here!"

I don't believe them

Until I reach down and feel the crown of a little head

Na.  I take a deep breath

And push, straining the blood vessels in my eyes

Holding my legs apart, away from a quivering pelvis

Chin pressed to chest

Ma.  And as if you and I are finally ready

You appear with a roaring cry

Animating every spirit in the room

Conveying a new zest to my soul

Some capable hands place you

Into my loving arms

And next to my heart

You feel

So at home

Sa. Ta. Na. Ma.

## Making Circles

The jeweler at the Christmas market
measures my fingers with a glance
focuses where a wedding band is absent

I try on some simple silver rings
for the fun of it, though I know
a ring doesn't measure
the expanse of my husband's love
or how we've carefully crafted
our adult lives around providing
a stable home for our two sons
who look up at us with the brightest eyes
the boys who want to love me so purely
until my owie booby is better

Anyways, rings wear different guises too
the way my husband's arms loop around my torso
when we're slow dancing in the kitchen
his breath on my neck, an incantation for healing

The ring of my 3-year-old's red magnifying glass
as he follows me into the bathroom and says
"Let me see if your hair is growing up"

I feel as if I'm not fulfilling my promise

I did say my hair would grow back

but I didn't tell him it will be

when the chemo sessions stop

when my cells get a chance to recuperate


He says I look like Doctor Strange

but means Sorcerer Supreme, portrayed

by Tilda Swinton in the Marvel movie

"Do you have superpowers?" he asks

"Are your hands spinning like this?"

he motions, turning his hands

in magic circles to open new dimensions


If it were only so easy, I'd channel mystical energy

walk through rings where time is fast forwarded

to the other side of this illness

## White Orchids

On my head, barely any hair
Spots of short brown peach fuzz
I put my wig on, social camouflage
So people don't have to wonder
Alopecia or cancer?

Hair loss – enough
But at least hair regrows
My left breast won't

I'm afraid to write
This journey scarcely touched
Must get past chemo fog

I buy white orchids
From the corner store
Place them by the window
A Drishti to hold my gaze
Something for myself

Life is a gift, a gift, a gift

## What a Wild Ride

It is windy, we are going to pick up
My mother-in-law from the airport
I say, "My hair is flying everywhere"
My three-year-old son says, "You mean your wig"

Later in the tub, I let him wash my wig
Propped on a Styrofoam head
He gently squeezes sponges full
Of water over the brown strands

Innocently he asks, "Can we wash
Oma's wig next?"

This task has become so ordinary to him
He imagines every woman
Has a wig to care for

## wishes wanting to be said

the body is a storyteller
I see in the bouquet of veins
and redness on my left breast
a discomfort seeking release

in my loss of hair and falling lashes
a sign I do not have to apologize
for my appearance, only pray
come scheduled surgery day

for an extraordinary event
for the tumor to respond enough
and shrink with each chemo session
so that the doctors and surgeons

will have a smaller margin of skin
and breast tissue to remove
is an intact nipple too much to ask for
I cast these questions away from my body

and inside me a nascent hymn

thrashes against an outcrop of basalt

columns, where once volcanic activity

birthed a wild seascape


and inside me so many wishes are

repeating to the shore, "lend me an ear"

# Glimpse Inside a Flower

(For Stephanie)

Sacred to me is
The way a flower blooms

You cannot force the bud
By bending her petals back

She will open when primed
On her own terms

A reminder to worry less
Slow down, live in the present

Other things in life grow
In this same pattern

Relationships, healing
Falling in love

# Some wounds will be slow to heal

Weeping from the pit of my stomach, I break

for the babes waking in Mariupol, Kyiv, Kharkiv

The news, a pie thrown in the face

victims struggle to see clearly

reach for something to clean up

and process the slight, the mess

Each city, an open mouth

raspberry red, bloody gums, extracted teeth

inhabitants know the meaning of war

carry their grief to a safe border

they should be the ones writing

Week after week I face cancer treatment

try to keep the tears quiet, try not to wake my sons

I feel what it's like to have poison affect the cells

feel grief destroy the body, feel either the earth

will envelope me or the sky will swallow me up

## Photo of My Breasts

Photography is the bringing to life
of an artistic vision with a viewfinder
the human process exposed in a single image

I expose myself to the nurses, the oncology
team and the plastic surgeons, a doctor
takes a photo for documentation
I begin humming with eyes closed
head leaning away from the lens, I know
these tears will belong to my survival story

They can all look at me, as I prepare
for the modified radical mastectomy, look
look, look before they try to take something
away, look, see this woman as a whole
at my strong shoulders, fierce bones
brave chest, a heart absorbing the light

I am bald and I am not ugly, look

I am going to lose my breast, look

all the while the music of life plays on

one pulled string after another

of course, there will be a symphony

within me still

after I've been cut

## To every woman facing breast cancer treatment

Dear Warrior, you are more than
what happens to your body on the outside
more than the bald head and pale face
that has fought through chemotherapy
more than flesh, breast tissue, lymph nodes
which have been removed to save you
woman with a soul so vast

I know those depths beneath the surface
where you accept the petal of skin
separated from donor site, offered to chest
I know newness you have to embrace
different on one side, bodies that look like mine
believe me, you will honor the petal
name the scar whatever, a bloom
magnolia, camellia, more delicate
badge stitched to your chest, symbol of life

I see in you the universe, yes
if we think we've lost everything
but something is left, that is
the most beautiful thing

Even a crystal doesn't do much in the dark

until you hold her up to the beauty of day

and watch her refract the light

rainbow after rainbow

## darkness attempts to share my pillow

run, run, run, but my legs will not take me
I wake up in the middle of the night and cry
now that I need to put off these peculiar notions
of reviving old griefs from my treatment's yesterdays

our goodbye at the gate was so strange, darkness and I
held hands and said things like, "will you stay in touch?"
then it walked out, and I crumpled behind
my stomach miserable after that tempter left
just a girl who allowed herself vulnerability
never knowing its influence on the way I felt

then, this trouble writing its electricity out of my body
the ghosts still summon me, of its hands around my…
its tongue softly pressing against my…

what did I leave but soft caresses?
what did I take but totems of its possession?
these are questions I ask in the quiet of night
when my mind grumbles unusual thoughts
to bring spirits back for moments

darkness, here is your poem, you devil, you brute

may our old passions flow away, like a cascade

on the move from some haunting enigma


taunt me no more in solitude, nor in dreams

leave my innermost landscapes unaltered

# Coming out of the shadows

As a precautionary measure the doctors
removed the axillary lymph nodes under
my left arm, along with my left breast
and when they pinched, stitched, and glued
me back together they left all kinds of pain
pain that feels like fishhooks under my skin
pain that makes me hunch down on one side

I cry in front of my physical therapist
it isn't easy to overcome the hurdles
in each physical therapy session
my mind must stop safeguarding self
in order to lift left arm overhead
regain my full range of motion

Tight, stubborn new skin on chest wall
that tenses has to be tensile as I reach out
little by little to the side, to the front, to the back
the goal is to reach over my head with ease
with a swinging motion, a high arabesque of sorts
like a fern waking up on the forest floor
unfurling effortlessly toward the light

Go away pain from stitches and scar tissue

in time I will raise the bar, stretch by stretch

and no longer flinch when asked to dance

to the pulsating dream songs of cleansing forest rain

yes, rain travels the map of an unsymmetrical

body without passing judgement

## Have Yourself a Sanguine Summer

Feeling fragile, a fuchsia

Turned upside down

As summer is perched

On the calendar, along

With pending treatments


Self-love becomes a chore

In the face of new medication

Add weeks of radiation therapy


I pick up the snotty tissue papers

Try to remain calm, try to let go

Untie the dressing gown in a cold room

Lay down on the bed, fill my lungs

With air as a machine whirs above me

Each breath a globe of hope

## Expressions and Marks

I'm not the only one who's been cut
And we all come undone when
Someone notices our scars, cracks, crevices. Surgery
Is not comfortable. Shape or form us
A healing process, so complex to navigate.
Some scars we like to keep
Others, we say, "I encourage you to fade."

We offer small comforts on scarring
"I am so proud of you for all the treatments
You have undergone, for being so positive
And such a warrior". We nurture ourselves
For a scar to take its final shape and color,
Love the skin, newly born on the scar line. Healing
With tender baby nerves and no radiation protection
About a year of no sun kisses
Add gentle light massages on the scar, surrounding tissues
Dabs of coconut oil and honey. The scars
Will take on an energy of cared for
And we can wear them proudly.

We share our experiences
Place our palms together

Holding in some emanating gleams

And from one bright spirit to the other,

We say, "They are really beautiful

Your streaks of light brown, pink brown

And pearly."

## These Days

I have stopped feeling lost or uncertain
about my life's path, I feel very much found
when I look at the incoming teeth
in baby Leopold's smile as he raises
dimpled fingers, pointing at all the marvelous
creations above his head, trees, birds
and clouds that hide airplanes

Then there are Viktor's eloquent questions
when he is acquiring conversational German
"Mommy, how do you say high five? What about
fist bump? What about sea monster?"
and I want to be around for a very long time
to help him learn the translations

I keep my hands open these days
and a backpack ready so that my two
awestruck boys who crawl or dance
around like each day is the most beautiful of all
will have space to keep noteworthy treasures
like fallen leaves, flowers, twigs, beach rocks
handfuls of sand, feathers, and old stickers

Even the stars they point at
will have a safe place to reside
if they ever choose to reach up
and pull one out of the sky

# Having a bottle at the park

Leopold the milk mouth makes a bed
with mama's scarf, a field of white
clover at his fingertips. Reach, baby
the world is yours, if I have anything
to say about it. I will fan the flame
of your dreams, even your tiniest hopes.
So young, yet already a symbol of light
touching forest finds in those chubby palms.

Bring awareness to the small, sublime
things, the honeybee's striped behind
poking out of a flower, great balls
of fiery red geraniums, like the ones
on your Oma's balcony in Bavaria,
or rice seeds humbly growing in paddies
where your Lola lives, on Panay island.

I tell you now, small things are special
they carry weight. The sound wind makes
when it wants to join you in a tent. Cicadas
conversing with their timbals at twilight,
crickets chirping with their elytra from crevices
in rocky crags. Sparrow visits on gloomy, gray

city sidewalks. Sand in the bathwater, remnants
of a spontaneous afternoon drive to the beach.

Reach, baby, for the magic in ordinary
bits and fragments of everyday life.

# Aloe Vera Nurturing

i.

Coming back to Bavaria feels special
the land welcomes me to my happy place
a premier spot for some rest and recuperation
I can see the Brauneck and Benediktenwand
just outside my in-laws' kitchen window


They are determined to put aloe vera
leaves on my leg overnight during our visit
the skin graft site glares at me when I wear
my lake shorts, the scar soon changes
with the homeopathic care, doesn't
look so fiercely red anymore


Papa Stephan sits at the table with a spread
of aloe vera leaves from the balcony
Mama Sabine has tape bandages
to hold the leaves in place
when I sleep, I get bandage wraps in
bubble gum pink or sapphire blue
signs that there is tenderness here

ii.

At home, four aloe vera plants

are delivered to my door, gifts

from Papa and Mama, I open

two leaves, put the gel on my scars

a continuation of their care

## Mama's Space, Mama's Way

In a few minutes two boys close their eyes
And are swiftly sound asleep, their peaceful
End of day grins hold me serendipitously
Tucking them in, a ceremonious routine

Sweet sleeping boys, tethered to me
With a bit of dream weaver thread
Strung with twinkling star beads
Picked out of the sky's blue bowl
And sun shimmer skimmed from the ocean
Just before the sun fell into the horizon

This is a mama speaking in code to disguise
The hard work that goes into running the show
A checklist for two matching shoes, car keys, wallet
Cleaning, always cleaning, washable markers
Are my saving grace, their inventor
Deserves his own public holiday

Now a baggy eyed mama bear, I tip toe
Away to enjoy the elegance of girl time
With an oat milk and lavender bath

Soaking in a swathe of suds and purple buds

I breathe in circles, orbiting around Oms

To slow my heart rate, let my chin rest

A collar of bubbly lace around my neck

# 27<sup>th</sup> of July 2022

The necklace falls against my collar bone

String of pearls from the Philippines

I press them in my palms, national gems each


Recent news about a 7.0 magnitude earthquake

In Northwestern Luzon whirls me

Home is all I can think about


Northbound roads blocked from landslides

Buildings cracked or tilted sideways

Millions of pesos/dollars in damage

To the nation's infrastructure


I draw comfort seeing friends giving

Updates on their social media platforms

Marked safe, another natural disaster

But I know these people, they'll pull together

"Bahala na," pick the pieces up, come what may


Overseas in Greystones I long for mangoes

Durian, rambutan, malunggay in my soup

I want to see my shadow on the sidewalk

A sampaguita heart in the center

# Embodiment

The page opens, the section reads
talking about cancer. I feel like a somebody
again, after a year of watching my life
from the outside of it. Family members took turns
to visit, helped with my children, cared for my home
saved me from social isolation.

My therapist says I should tell my boys honestly
about the cancer that was in my body, then
they won't invent their own versions
of why I was in and out of the hospital.

Do I have to tell my kids anything?
Only if they ask questions. My four-year-old asks,
"Is the hole in your owie boobie almost gone?
I don't want to see it." Part of the scar runs
under my armpit, peers out of sleeveless shirt.
"Can you wear a shirt, like with these, with sleeves?"

I witness events in chronological time but feel
emotions at random. Part of the female experience
is to be honest with the self, even when difficult
journeys affect a relationship with the body. I'm not

a candidate for reconstructive breast surgery, the wound
too close to chest wall for a silicone implant, physique
too lean to offer fat and tissue for reconstruction. Maybe
I don't want to undergo more surgeries anyway.

Part of the mothering experience is recovering
trust. If I wear a prosthesis it will be as if
it never happened but acknowledging that it did.

And what about the wife aspect? This is the hardest
part to navigate after treatment and surgery. I am
a flute, my husband's hands and mouth don't know
how to play my tune. Intimacy in the bedroom becomes
hard to unlock. I don't want to take my bra off, I have
a sensitive, conservative concept of my figure now. My
husband kisses my right breast, while his hands and gaze
avoid my flat left side, but I want him to touch my scar, feel
the pounding in my chest. Tell me I am a vixen in perfect skin.

## Post-Surgery Screening of Myself

it's the first day of August, five months since excision of tumor
and breast, I scan the mirror at times, recall winter months treatment
when I lost my ability to daydream, strange how illness feels
like fiction, alters looking forward to the future with one's family
now I wait to see less nurses in blue scrubs, soon no more
routine blood tests, I count down to the last pokes in my arm
nearing the mid-way point for six months of chemo tablets

it's the first day of August, I'm home with my boys
indulging in long lazy cuddles on the sofa, showering wondrous
balcony plants tucked into potting soil with plastic water guns
seasonal blooms still about, spells of splendor, still time
to enjoy the blue globe thistles, sunflowers, hollyhocks
still time to greet the sunrise birds in song

it's the first day of August, I'm kissing my husband to taste
summertime ambrosia on warm lips, we strive to be more present
open-eyed, who we are inwardly, nourishing our connection
we did say in sickness and in health, babe, inherently yielding
to the feeling our hearts are fuller and lighter to carry
all at the same time, we accept change, a new lease on life
an uprooted orchid replanted, a place to put down roots

# Holding It Together

This August the boys seem to grow up too fast

We dress Viktor in lots of polo shirts

In preparation for his new school year

Leopold chatters expertly, learns bears say roar

Crawls and growls, going around the house


Summer slips away on blown dandelion seeds

Then I take Viktor to school on his scooter

He cruises past me, one hand on the handle

"Rock and roll, baby", he's almost too cool

To hold my hand now, crossing the street

Leopold tries to imitate everything we do

Blows drool kisses and claps his hands

Chuckles at shapes going into the shape sorter


These boys have big laughs like playful ocean splashes

That make up for all the laundry I have to hang

The clotheslines adorned with little monster socks

Washcloths, bibs, small outfits next to each other

I want to make these boys happy forever
Give them pain au chocolat picnics in gardens
Have play dough tea parties on rainy days
Watch the sun shimmer across the ocean
As it looks for sleep beyond the horizon

I pull them closer for prolonged mama caresses
Hold them the way waves always want the shore

# 9th Margaret

Aunt Daisy, helps me gather family data
I absorb like a sponge, we send emails
and snail mail, she has my poetry books
sends encouraging messages about my work
she gifted me a piece of family history
a 19th century Scottish coin silver plate
passed on from her maternal grandmother
my great grandmother emigrated
from Scotland with her family
to Newfoundland, then to New York City
where she met and married Howard Lewis
that's where my father got his first name

When I carry the plate in my hands
I feel our Scottish roots, early emblems
folk songs and dances at a cèilidh
bagpipes and fiddles in the breeze
it is an honor to know, to understand
the connection to distant ancestors
the importance of heirlooms

# David di Michelangelo

At the Victoria and Albert Museum, this man

of muscle and marble is just a replica

but his tall stature brings a glow to my eyes


Michelangelo's thoughts chiseled in marble

to make a body, desired as it is, masculine

details hold my dancing pupils

crown of curls, cupid's bow

taut torso, almost pulsing veins


I stand at his plinth, like a doll

amongst the stardust that floats

around the nape of his neck

human nature is always itself

and I wonder what paths of caprice

moved in Michelangelo's hands

to expose and refine David's particles


I write on my bucket list, must see original

at La Galleria dell'Accademia, for my soul

to be pinched, as if I could make his marble

mouth smile, upturn his stern countenance

pass through impenetrable eyes, give him

something to remember me by

ignite the torch again, Andiamo

a Firenze, onward to Florence, Italy

# I know this early autumn rain

today we stay indoors
as the rain taps on windows
asking "Where to now?"

we're not the same youths
who scampered around
with waterproof ponchos
up and down Sagada hillsides
looking for strawberry wine
before retreating into our cabin
at St. Joseph Resthouse, when
you asked maybe for the fourth time
if I would marry you

did you know then, Mr. wind-tousled hair
and misty gray eyes, peaking
over Paulo Coelho's The Alchemist
what you were getting yourself into

the rain passes the window
of our house, calling our footsteps
seaward or cliff-ward

changed slightly by parenthood

two boys snuggle between us now

we are happy to be indoors, held like

pomegranate seeds pressed in

a pink blanket on the sofa

# A Mailbox Near the Mountains and Wishful Thinking

we feed into one another
have dreams together
after a journey around the world
we'd like a permanent address to get
my favorite poets in the mailbox
his manuals for home activities

space for his hot tub and sauna too
a studio for my artistic pursuits

we wish we could name an acre of land
near a mountain, with a water source
ocean, river, or lake where some produce
herbs, flowers can be plucked year round
in a yard or sunroom, extra room too
for our children and their children to visit

show us that acre, name the price

# By Way of Ireland

The road that guided me to you? I've partly come

Because I need to find the pieces of myself

I rarely address, distracted day by day


Who made the first move? Somewhere

Along my search for a poetic destination

You called out to me in photographs


Your landscapes make blackout poetry

The words come out like imagist

Paintings, winding backroads

That authentically capture emotions

Moments that keep us connected


I want to cruise on these postcard roads

Until I know every scenic overlook by name

Hands out of the car window

Air rushing against my cheeks

Gusting through my hair, old playmate

Suddenly reintroduced


Your face so engrained in my mind

I can reach out to touch you anytime

And I wonder if it will be enough

To love you vigorously, in brief

Then who, when I am gone?

## More

Ireland is full of poems on stones unturned
I dreamt once that I wanted to be where
the land meets the sea, so I convinced
my husband to take the job, pay cut and all
he hasn't decided if he's forgiven me yet
thinking we didn't make the right decision
how naïve of me to believe I could have
my dream life at no extra cost
how different our experiences were
upon moving here, he saw the clouds as
heavy, full of rain, I heard only folk songs
*Will ye go, lassie, go?*

Is this his luck for marrying a poet, a woman
sensitive to subtle energy who goes about kicking up
stones and longing for a stronger earth-connection
in a place like Greystones, wandering north beach

Somedays I plead with him, let me tell you about
the phenomenal mixed lighting on rainy days
sunrays spilling through cumulonimbus
blankets that get your soul perked up and tickled
salutations from the sky that inspire creativity

Yes, sometimes it's lonely, I'll admit, being away
from family and friends, but they too will come
when they're ready for a quieter kind of beauty
like the rain that pulls hardened hillwalkers
to the cliff walk, precipitation on coats, on glasses
but it makes them feel empowered

Yes, sometimes our little world needs
more of what is empowering
*Will ye go, lassie, go?*

## Standing in the Tide

Greystones waves are serendipitous
starting somewhere beyond the sand
where contemplations are born in water
turquoise, aquamarine, lapis lazuli

Today— a blank page in a journal
someone who found a muse in the sea
recommends sea swimming, even though
this water is cold all year round

This old soul glows like a painting
with knowing, the creases of the shore
on her hands, the ocean's pulse in her steps
she says this water was meant for me

Sea swimming turns strangers to friends
like sea glass scattered about, smoothed
by tides only to resurface, shimmering
its importance differs to each of us

I do not want to lose my silicone
prosthesis, I pull it out of my swimsuit
and tuck it into my beach bag
one must be adaptable around water

I think I get it now, something about sea
swimming blurs into the essence of a woman
if there is water around us, acceptance
re-enacts itself everywhere

# Synesthesia in County Kerry

At a Killarney inn, I woke

a reclined silhouette

trying to ask my body questions

meditating, mountain outlines

planting orchids in my mind

inside a commotion of weary blues

trying to find something concrete

in the chaos of change

otherwise unnoticed

trying to take part

when all the art and pain

wanted to come out of my body


Then I spent time with creative

women, craved their feminine energy

Eleanor drove me and another Sara

to the Paps of Anu, each summit

had a prehistoric cairn

they looked like nipples

a babe could feed from

I smiled as we approached

Eleanor got into character
performing artist, personifying
Morrigan, holding ceremonial distaff
wearing fierce mask, well-made, she had
survived, phoenix from a studio fire

Our next stop was Ross Island
where the other Sara said
we should hug a tree
and a pine called out
to my longing arms
flakes of sunshine on its bark
formations, peace offerings

I wondered what to leave behind
but I knew the uneven terrain
didn't ask anything of us
only that we take a closer look
exchange a nurturing touch

# I See You in Wildflower Blooms

It's not like me to dwell on what lies here, what lies
beyond, but the Wicklow Mountains made me think of you
how you've gone enticed by the upland winds, growing steadily
ascending, only visiting in dreams, when I dream you've woken
up from your coma or you've sat up in your grave
and it was all a mistake that we buried you

I sit here, cross-legged posture, cocooned in rainy day mist
barely managing to take charge of my solitary breaths
so I get up to stretch legs turned tingly, shakily skirt along
the beach of Upper Lake Glendalough, wonder if you are now
intertwined with the persistent light that touches ripples
on the lake, light that plays on the soft rolling waves

Or perhaps you're in the soil's minerals I dust off my pantlegs

in fragments of dirt stuck between rubber lugs on my trail shoes

all this and yet you still belong to the expansiveness

of the mountains, iridescent summits not too far away


Perhaps you're also joined to the trills and churrs in a skylark's

song living in the subtlest cadences, the reverberating hum

of music that envelopes the yellow gorse and purple heather

the melody on the hills as I drive along – not really gone

## Stargazer's Canticle

This song is for the man I used to call
when my road was forked in wildernesses
on weary starlit nights, seeking some
divine truth when I couldn't decide between
the short way or the detour, left or right
he would tell me how his own revelation
occurred, how his life changed for the better
after moving to the Philippines where he met
my mother, their lives well lived, all worth it
to have a beautiful girl they almost named Princess
but settled more appropriately with Sarah Joy
I'd laugh on the phone just hearing his voice
hoping he'd hear me out before I lost reception

He constantly said he believed in me, would continue
to believe whether I called from Alaska or Timbuktu
whether I became a teacher or a folksinger
just as long as I called home from time to time

I still write melodies for this man, his smile
the hems of some old familiar home
when I go stargazing, reaching for star dust songs
that whisper reasoning to my disquieted soul

the man who would have lived much longer

if our love could have healed him

he would have said, "Show and tell

it all, baby doll. Show and tell it all."

## No Shortsighted Man

Cataracts and glaucoma blurring your sight, you still perceived
the world better than I did. A visionist, eyes opened or shut
you viewed humankind as sentient, sensed characteristics
in people, in surroundings. You chose a habitat, Benguet province
the mountains and the people. You didn't like to drift far from
that comfort zone, memorizing roads all over the Cordillera.
I craved bigger cities. To see like you, I had to become
unladen by limitations, premature opinions. You had seen
more mornings, days giving birth to new days, a span
of life not wanting to die out. Every day you woke up
early, thanking the evening that had passed, greeting
sunbeams over the rim of a coffee cup, Benguet beans
or blend of arabica, secret formula.

I accompanied you on a flight to Celena's wedding
so you could walk her down the aisle, dance as
a father giving away his daughter. We had a layover
in Guangzhou, China. You said, "Don't walk so fast
I can barely see you in the crowd, just a blur of your
blue sweater". I thought, "Hurry up, keep up with me
old man. Our departure gate is right there."

Now I can't ask you to forgive me for being hasty, always

rushing then. You'd be proud of me though, I am

learning how to slow myself down, how to stop

smell flowers. I put plant clippings in my pocket

lavender, rosemary. I ask my soul questions. I pray.

## call me a survivor, memorable, always

made from more than a heap of memorable breaths
I can be this raw with you, I can fall into your arms

open hands, palms placed on the table, we
swallow aphrodisiacs, they hit our blood hard

almost a year since my diagnosis, jumping through
hoops, needles, needles, needles in my skin, primary IV
bags, secondary IV bags, drip chambers, tubing
mourning the lost breast, preventative care insight
for the next few years, we want to put the months
of my sickness far behind us, rejoice in remission

I gnaw on your wrists, corn on a cob
bones and strength, you are found
between my lungs, beat of my ballad
eyes closed, lips pressed upon my mouth

hallowed be thy unpretentious love
no need to explain the principle of Ubuntu
hold me in tender repose, I am because you are
you are because I am, water and clay molded
together, finding courage, comfort, you me one

# Recognition

Moving around the globe
the deepest, most intimate
drifting away from places
I am searching, and yet
I've found my definition
of intimacy

We see each other
the way we love
he; a parallel street
I can watch and bloom
traversing my inner child
it is strange to have had
a home far away
my personal history
a colorful one
developed photos
in my palm

I write in between
bursts of strength
feeling empathy
understanding what is
said, not said

We give to each other
what we want
a measure
of self-care
new home
close enough
he; my city
my holy grail

## The Hair We Wear

The ego in my hair was taken back
a notch, the one that used to push out
bobby pins when I had fatigued my arms
in a fight to neatly pin it up
the colicky baby that used to make
my head hot and livid in my sleep
midnight wake up calls to pat my sweat

Now it's boy short, a different beast
of burden, chemo curls, uncontrollable
but I like the way it's too easy to clean
economical with shampoo and conditioner
air dries in about 15 minutes after a wash

I've enjoyed watching it grow back
going from a brand-new, bald babe
to a woman with newfound confidence
baldness became the least of my
worries when I ate each spoonful
of humility avoiding my reflection
in the hospital room, post-surgery
needing assistance to use a bed pan
then to go to the toilet or take a shower

trying not to wet the special bandages
negative pressure wound therapy

The VAC bag gurgling at my side
tube pulling fluid from my wound
the daytime nurse humored me
"I see you've got your Gucci bag"

When I got enough strength to go
from my bed to the stairwell, I saw
my bald reflection in the windows
imagined mining for inner beauty
unveiled glamour, a pageant queen
walking the stage, waving to the audience

## Love poems double back

The first thing I recognized as poetry was
a letter I wrote at 4 years old, to my parents
it read, "I love you, mommy and daddy"
mom taught me love's meaning, feeding me at birth
dad guided me to travel, songs of the open road
my siblings introduced me to soul connections
the idea of sharing a sister's or brother's happiness
nature instructed me to listen to the planet's energy
how little acts of mindfulness can go a long way

And still, what I recognize as poetry is having
two boys who prove every day how my pen
came full circle, boys who look up and call me mama
with love-filled eyes, boys who put faith in me
like Bodhisattvas placed on the earth to bring
a sense of home, a sense of enlightenment

# For my small scholars of truth

Today I am here with you and that
is what matters
right here, right now
live every moment
to the fullest

Let your hearts
take command often
give and get the best
from life
mend pain, mend fears

In your endeavors
set goals, put your passion
and energy toward them
dream, have so many dreams
trivial or complex

If you must cast shade
on another being
choose the sun scorched
offer a drink
of water for rehydration

If you must tease
choose cold waves
with your pantlegs
rolled up, for you are
fiercer than the storm

If you must toil
choose worthy causes
work with intention
aim for your mark
go the distance

I once heard
two shorten the road
because a loved one's support
makes the road
more manageable

Walk determinedly
in the light of love
as brothers
boys with hope, resilience
a sense of belonging

## Sibling Seas

There is a structure in the sand we've
formed with collected seashells,
a heart, sandwiched between
the letter "I" and the letter "U".
A message my two young sons
cannot decipher yet. "How is a seashell
made?" my 5-year-old asks. I research
soft-bodied mollusks have a hard outer
layer with specialized cells to build up
a protective structure. It consists of
tiny proteins and calcium carbonate
to protect the organism living inside.
The outer shell is rough, hard to
break. The inner shell is soft, we call it
mother of pearl.

I wish to be like a seashell today,
for my outer layers to protect me from
the elements, from the world that is
so unbearable sometimes, from people
who don't know their words

have the power to crack me open,

"Feel free to live your best life

without me... I'm not going to reply

anymore". Yet, I also wish for more of

my softness to be exposed, my heart

that can be so fragile but also life-

giving. I long to be kind enough so

that when others gaze into me, they

marvel at my storm tossed vehicle

and how I've endured the journey.

My sons begin fighting over a bucket.

The 5-year-old wants to fill it with

shells, the 1-year-old wants to put

handfuls of sand inside and dump it

out. I want to tell them not to fight.

Sibling fights become more painful

as you get older. I've gotten to this

point by keeping my ears open to my

sister's pain and holding my tongue.

Language does not repair or fix

anything, "Are you frustrated with me? I thought you wanted to banish me as your sister". Language is just air, but we expect so much from it.

## Autumnal Instincts

October has crept upon us, and we welcome insulated coats
ready to face colder temperatures with the promise
of walking outdoors, hand in hand, finding
solace in forests, holding up those showy leafy crowns
red, orange, brown, reaching skyward in one last dance
before their talk goes muted by cold
that calls for rest, hibernation

And aren't we so much like falling leaves
summer still pulsing in our eardrums, reverberating
in our chests, the echoing beats inside us

May we transition gracefully into this new season
make dance effortless, body talk painless
take nature in again, out of necessity
allowing in the mist of early morning
autumn flower songs pouring out of us
chrysanthemums, begonias, dahlias
spending slower moments feeling their essence

## Showing up in blurs

Oh, O! O for October's end,
the day of the dead approaching. I go
looking for marigolds, bright colored
flowers for the ofrenda. I should paint
pictures of loved ones lost
to let them know we still remember.

But remembering is for the living,
our way of coping, an altar built for holding
them again, temporarily.

I don't even know what to place
on the altar, there is not space enough
for all the memories. I watch the rain
instead. Water makes us look
rippled and layered, we forget
our weight in it.

And what about the rain that floods
our thoughts? What does it carry away
when it has passed? Remembrances
above the land just washed –
our minds clearing up
after the storm.

# Beer cans and bottles under bushes

------- beer can --------
living in a digitally
inclined world is high
speed monotony on
repeat mankind's
inventions weigh
more than plants and
animals combined
reducing our environ-
mental impact feels
trickier every day
with societal urges to
consume never mind
the fact that we could
all live with less stuff
never mind every
living thing has a spirit
why is the common
shape for recycling
three arrows that chase
each other
signifying our efforts
to be more eco-friendly
to reduce our carbon
footprint yet these

efforts sometimes feel
futile for my species
dumbfounded full
of passive contentment
homo sapiens but we
don't do enough for
the comfort of our
only home still we're
trying to escape a
hamster wheel that
we're all rotating
toward destruction
over the edge

-------- bottle --------

when the noise of the

world makes my ears

ring with the tinnitus

of chaos and I feel too

frail to go on writing tell

these ears that I can't

change horses in the

middle of the race can't can't

can't turn around and run

180 degrees in the opposite

direction can't even retreat

because my true self mapped

out every possible hideaway

I could go tell these ears

I need to connect to my breath

teach me how to play *Blowin'*

*in the Wind* on the ukulele

one string at a time until

I come around and find

reasons to celebrate positive

climate news cities banning

toxic forever chemicals from

clothing and food packaging

entire nations addressing
pollutants prohibiting single-
use plastics the ozone layer's
chance for recovery

## So, You Wanted a Muse

Is it gibberish to confess
You are my ancient city
On a hill, the gold leaf gilding
The rough edges of my life
The agave syrup swirled in my bowl
Of breakfast grains, chia seeds, berries
On my mind like citrus, tangerine peels
The juicy flesh I eat to reach the seed of you
Pulp and fluid, an ongoing ocean gurgling
Flirtatious words, sonnets at sunset

I search for you in the dark
Like a perfume bottle, familiar
Shape kept in the center console
Of my car, open up this vehicle
And I will sing to you those healing songs
That help you carry the weight of falling
Into another person's spell
Take me home to wear the spray of you
Glistening around my collarbone

How can I convince you to look for nectar

On my lips only, give to me in a voice uncontrived

The prehistory of a springtime kiss

For when you kiss me dear

Your sighs want to live in my voice

You make me sing, ventriloquist

## Paris Heart Sounds

I had trouble falling asleep, knowing the streets
of Paris were beneath my hotel window
the murmuring voices, the whoosh of verses
a turntable hour around midnight calling to me
reminding me to let go of self-eroding fears
my fears were not my fee into the city

Then in the morning I went sightseeing
stood under Arc de Triomphe and felt
like I should slough off the old ways
no need to construct walls
but archways of peace, because
this city is resilience revived
this city is walking up steps
with broken wings, soaring again
the world unfolding

Paris, Paris, my lungs chanted
breathing all of her in
French songs resonating
from heart to tongue's tip

I made my way, reluctantly to the airport
au revoir, fare thee well, dear Paris
we can never be certain when or where
we will have our next embrace

## anything she desires

now here, a soul in transit, a hybrid product
occasionally seeking to touch base with my roots
mixed heritages inherited, a hodge-podge
of features only God could have handpicked
the ability to be fair skinned in the winter
and copper toned at the peak of summer
singing all the national anthems from places
I've learned to keep with me

oftentimes I feel like making sense of my quirky
personality that came with the package, coming to
terms with my world views is frequently addressed
while roaming streets of old cities, new to me
filled with eagerness to see the best cityscapes
spending days to their maximum potential
walking, eating, sight-seeing, chatting
sipping mugs of fresh conversation and syntax

I want to know what the locals do, more informative
than my Tripadvisor app or travel websites
the story wouldn't be complete otherwise
with a friend to be my tour guide, the world
becomes a classroom, we are both

students and teachers absorbing culture
interchanging thoughts, opinions
exchange students on this planet

so it is the same with me, the heritage I possess
does not necessarily need to be scrutinized
or placed under a microscope, it plays a role
in viewing the world from multiple sides
of the spectrum, and when I step through
this world striving to love and understand others
wholeheartedly, there is less questioning
of myself or which side I belong on

## Last pills of Capecitabine and the art of inwardness

feeling overwhelmed was part of
losing parts of me, first the hair
then the left breast, all this loss
a role in the awakening of who I am
my loving and intelligent self

I'm done with the tough treatments
goodbye to the days I would dress up
for my chemotherapy sessions
scarves, black pointy boots, wheeling
the IV pole to the restroom, touching up
lipstick, envisioning, a stronger self
the way one holds on to a bouquet
of flowers aging in a vase
stargazer lily and rose centerpieces
losing petals, droopy leaves turning yellow
still picking out the old fillers, dry, brown
rearranging the sparse flowers
diligently refilling the water

so much importance in the process
today I remember the essentiality
of meditation, silence, breath
discovering medicine within
sacred, everlasting ceremony of life

time to celebrate, say thanks to all those
who gave me wings on this journey
their hard work could not go unnoticed
steady working rhythm, clockwork of saints

what tokens of gratitude can I leave
with them, many thanks, many thanks
many thanks

## Gratitude's Expanse

In Venice I want souvenirs
made in Italy, I purchase
a handmade silk scarf, dusty rose
leather gloves, cashmere lining
they make me feel like
once again, time is flitting
and all around, life is
a walk in the park
*Thank you*

Seeing my reflection
in shop windows near
Campanile di San Marco
it's as if I had rarely seen
myself before, I am forced
to admit there is so much pleasure
now knocking inside me, this space
this city is like standing in the center
of a queen conch, that translates
the ocean's dulcet tones
wonders abounding
*Thank you*

Enchanted, I hop on a gondola

with my husband and sons

by Ponte di Rialto, wade through

water ways, movie sets

caught unawares by beauty

dreams in a constellation heart

shine in my rib cage

urging me to open wider

*Thank you*

## Daylight Saving Time

Dawn performs her unapologetic routine
And we set our clocks back, reluctant
To face Sunday morning

In this season, Sun is shuffling
Toward the southern horizon
Night prepares for longer spells
Of mischief, stocking up
Black treacle, molasses
Wood ash, charcoal, soot
Cauldrons overspill sticky pigments
That settle into northern skies

But Day is a patient maiden
Who brings powdered chalk
Gathers petals, lilac, baby blue
Mixes them with dewy drops
To wash away the doings
Of her sister's nocturnal artistry

They carry on like this
A constant significance
To each other

## Entering Nostalgic Places

i.
Dad is absent, swapped with sadness
in my chest, a forlorn spirit that grows
tired of swallowing grief, there are days
his loss makes me too queasy

To carry on, and I attempt to pray
for those I love, have loved, have room
still, to love, I revisit what I know
of goodness and truth

Learn to make amends for hurting
anyone in my nuclear family
my extended family, the members
I don't talk about or talk to

ii.
There are days I wait for shifts in the cosmos
that will alter the sad endings
perfect bound stories of the depressed
displaced, abused, ill-treated

And I wonder who will embrace the girl
on a Native American reserve, cooped up
in her own homeland, no Independence Day to celebrate
her language a ghost, echoing through canyons

The street children in the Philippines, outstretching
their palms for meager pesos by day and huddled
on cardboard boxes near overpasses at night
sleep interrupted by the rumble of engines whirring on

The young women in Iran veiled by a silent tapestry
who court danger by letting their hair down
the boys in Yemen trading their innocence
for the weight of a rifle's fractured dreams

Can someone, anyone, revise the life cycles
of stolen childhoods and homes destroyed
by the greed and senselessness of war
for everywhere there are mothers

Under hazy skies holding their babies who
will no longer grasp hands or bounce balls
babies without limbs, babies going
nighty night in the ground

iii.
If dad were still here, how would he
weigh in on the confusion, unrest I feel
would he shake his head, offer some advice
to convince me humanity is not collapsing

Perhaps it's better that he left in his sleep
as to not wake up to a world like this
where so many of us are half asleep
half fighting for redemption

Would he say, be a pen, even
one that screams in the shadows
believe, believe, believe
there are days we can do better

# Fourth Thursday of November

A reverie can last one car ride long
On the way to the department store
Hands propped up on the steering wheel
A receiving place, nothing up my sleeves
I try to manage quiet contemplations
Counting my conveniences, I list
The privileges, the ability to purchase
New underwear, shampoo, soap, groceries
Clean my clothes in a washing machine
Access to kitchen appliances, electricity
Three meals a day, soft pillows, large bed
To sleep in comfortably, a stock of
Sanitary napkins in my bathroom
A passport to cross borders
Safely, without harassment
In one piece, some 21$^{st}$ century
Girls are not so lucky

I want to climb up a mountain

With a zip lock bag of gratitude

Spill it in the wind and wish

For it to travel across oceans

Then come back, softened

With care and deliberation

Expanded by the voyages wherein

Nothing is taken for granted

## Shells

I haven't been to a tropical beach
since the pandemic started
sometimes I think of Siargao's
warm climate, waters surrounded
by snorkeling spots, ocean lagoons
coves lined with silent bangka boats

I went to her sandy shore once
carrying a sarong and ukulele in my tote
settled in a perfect spot to study
shells, the outlines of the coast
I tried to make a game plan in case
the tide crept up to my sandy outpost

Then I wandered to the water's mouth
in one fell swoop it cooled
my tender scars, washed my body, this
body that's faced the harsh
elements of girlish fears and anxiety

And the tide took me, red eyed, drippy nosed
and told me to dance in tropical showers
to reconnect with my breath
I wasn't sure how to cope with such
beauty then, waves splashing in strength
speaking what keeps us alive, swim, swim
through rough times, swim all the while

## Scenarios of Feeling Small

one wound that hasn't healed, continues to reopen
is my love-hate relationship with the Philippines
pearl of the orient, holds the world's largest pearl
I treasure snapshots of scenic beaches, luscious green
mountain provinces around the country
that brought me into existence, my roots still
in the soil there, but with all its beauty comes
the pain, the persistent inequality, cavernous gap
between the rich and the poor, the ignored images
of slum children in makeshift homes near rubbish heaps
no water to wash the grime off their shoeless feet

some days I imagine my face underwater
seeing a coral reef for the first time
blissfully chasing parrot fish, diving down
for closer glimpses of the easy-going marine life
then the sun disappears, the fish scatter and hide
the reef changes from dazzling
purple, orange, and pink to an uninviting drop-
off, storm clouds fog up my snorkeling mask

I get cramps in my calves, unable to swim
to safety, the shoreline becomes unreachable
alone in a vast ocean, the current is taking me
breathless I wave my arms to signal
lifeguards who look on, choose not to see

## Refrains for the Giving Season

This holiday we are bringing our sons
To their Oma's and Opa's house
In Bavaria, the burning wood stove
Will continue throughout the day
Casting warm auburn glows

Ready, there, the children will all
Know that it's… it's… it's Christmas

But somewhere in a crowded city
Manila or Cebu, street kids are
Caroling for coins and handouts
With makeshift instruments
Foraged from rubbish dumps
Rattles of rocks in plastic bottles
Soda caps on strings, tin can drums
Bamboo percussion, hungry beats

Listening to them sing
Blameless voices, knocking on
Car windows at the red lights
Stopping shoppers outside malls
*Ang Pasko ay kay saya*

I want to dig for pocket change

Check my bank account

Is there enough to send to

A foundation, a charity

To buy them presents

*Sa araw ng pasko*

I'm sure my children won't mind

Paying it forward, our feelings

In a snow globe, shaken up

To spread glittery happiness

Around us now, Christmas at last

I got it! Catch

## Zugspitze, Top of Germany

you know me, know my ecstasy is mountains
where I'm happier, a participant of this planet
listening to your nervous words on the gondola
responses just bubble up inside, carrying signs
instructions to be patient, unfiltered, soft with you

here's where we push up old glass ceilings
melt your acrophobia by warm talk
conducting steam that could heat
a sauna, power a thermal bath
ceremony that makes my eyes too cloudy
all I can see is the mountains and you
incapable of movement, speech

you would do this for me, to satiate
my sensation-seeking mountain habits
ich liebe dich, the motor pulls us along
ich liebe dich, my heart glides up the cables

# On the way to somewhere

I am a talking bird
made to catch the roots
of day anew

Here, winter performs
a little silvery prance
the field is frosty, halted
again, in morning peace
I attempt duets
with ice-rimmed flowers
chords wave white
words shimmer
on the edge
of last leaves

I smile at some trees
loosened from the soil
that avoided being burned
in the holiday hearth

Time falls open
taking last year's
calendar off the wall
and this season says
just try your best
remember practicing
your song that tells a story
might be something good

My heart unburdened
singing becomes enough
to spark a winter fire

Synchronicity waits beyond
movements, spring's return
is in the air
whispering prayers
I fly away to you

## Kindness Seen

Glued to a computer, you've been working overtime
and I want to wash out the stains of stress
you wear in your shirt. Hem the threads
coming undone, remind you of waiting
with eyes wide open, adrenaline rushing
through your chest. At points in time
wherein you waited for your family,
and dreamt of children
who would bare your kind heart.

When you are consumed by the stress,
yield to your breath. It has longed to expand
your inner spirit one transcendent inhale
after another. Put aside the clamor of work
and find agreement in yourself, not perfection.

This life doesn't require your slavish obedience
to some code of behavior. Learn to take the weight
off your feet, take every step in stride,
take no more than what you require.

For a friendly reminder we can rewatch
*Baraka,* as the short ruptures of silent footage

subsequently shift our emotions. Serene
landscapes, monks chanting in earnest,
elaborately decorated temples juxtaposed
with the unpleasant underbelly of capitalism,
landfills that taint the fringes of Calcutta,
assembly lines of workers robotically
manufacturing cigarettes and electronics.

As these social cries rush through our minds
verifying countless wrongs to make right,
numerous paths to fulfill society's needs,
we can continue watching in the dark
until the footage imparts so many people
in the world are in fact interwoven. The same
seeking of sages, lighting of candles, fading out.

Then let us pull away from our computers
which hold no adequate explanation
for the human path. Let us turn our attention
to the right places where all around love
has no single form and to be kind is priceless.

## Dip Deeper

In intervals of 5-10 seconds
He presses finger on shutter
*Taking photo*

I can gesticulate freely
Remove my layers
And he does not judge
My creative process
*Taking photo*

We set up a self-timer
He removes his shirt
The goosebumps
Rise on his skin
To meet the cold room
He joins his hands with
Mine, to seek warmth
*Taking photo*

We dance a little
And become blurs
In slow exposure settings
Finding movement to express
A sweet sort of daydream
*Taking photo*

## In Savasana

Somewhere in the liminal period
between illness and healing there is
so much seeking of remedy. Words

enter the mouth and become
intentions that travel
to the rest of the body. I relax

flat on my back, bring one hand
to the left side of my chest, where
the lemon-sized tumor

was removed. I notice the firmness
of this flat surface against my palm
and strike up a conversation. Hello,

left breast. Thank you for everything
you've done for me. For allowing
me to nurse my first son

for a year and a half. For providing
a pillow when my second son
came into this world, although

I could not nurse him. For fulfilling
your purpose and making me
a complete woman. My dear,

left breast, to let you go was a lifesaving
procedure. Just think about
what I got back after losing you.

## Offering of Dance

Body of land, body land, land body
See the floor as partner, it will catch
So tell your sisters not to weep
For your wounds, you
Have what it takes to release
The trauma of your story's underbelly
Search the internet for "beautiful
Body" and scroll, but if there is no
Resonating image, see your
Body as reference, fulfilling recovery

Be the child with skidded knees
And come to the dance anyways
Be the woman with one breast
And yes, absolutely come to the party
The stressed mother of young ones
The daughter grieving her lost father
For the enigma that is you
Yes, yes, yes, the floor
Can bear your weight, cradle, support

You've sat silent under the veil of grief
And now the cocoon opens
And here I am, I know this woman
Who holds songs and dreams

Our bodies are survivor stories

Our hearts are pumping as our legs

Pump to the rhythm of our breath

Let our movement be secret telling

The dance – resistance

# Acknowledgments

*Uprooted Orchid* has truly been a passion project, reframing my experience of grief and emphasizing the journey of healing, resilience, and hope. I thank my beautiful family who held me up during this period in my life, the doctors and nurses who saw me through treatment, and the support groups and friends that helped me manifest the light in dark times.

I'd also like to thank my publisher, Edward Vidaurre, for seeing potential in this poetry collection, "This collection is a second chance at healing and living and forgotten prayer." Thanks to my thesis director, Andrea Cote-Botero for asking me all the right questions as I prepared the bulk of this work for my thesis project while I pursued my MFA in Creative Writing at the University of Texas at El Paso.

**A Tent Pitched Near the Guadalupe River** appeared in "Texas Poetry Calendar, 2022"

**Autumnal Instincts** was featured in "A Flow of Words", Scariff Bay Community Radio, November 2022

**Coming out of the shadows** was shared on "The Resilience Within" with Joyous Windrider Jimenez

**Expressions and Marks** and **On Vincent Cooper's "Zarzamora"** appeared in "Driving into Black Mountains"

**Forests Born Under Sky Dreams, True Like Time**, and **Waiting for Winter** appeared in "Boundless 2021", the official anthology of the Rio Grande Valley International Poetry Festival

**On Breath and Birth** appeared in "The Everyday, the Mundane, and the Brave"

**Reclaiming the Narrative** appeared in "Reconnecting to the Body Chapbook"

**Visiting My Ilongga Mother** appeared on savesellshenel.com

www.ingramcontent.com/pod-product-compliance
Lightning Source LLC
Chambersburg PA
CBHW031525120626
46545CB00005B/2005